SAMUEL
ADAMS
PATRIOT AND STATESMAN

SPECIAL LIVES IN HISTORY THAT BECOME

Signature LIVES

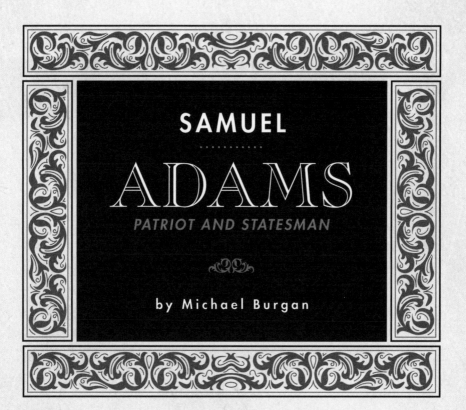

SAMUEL

ADAMS

PATRIOT AND STATESMAN

by Michael Burgan

Content Adviser: Richard J. Bell,
History Department,
Harvard University

Reading Adviser: Rosemary G. Palmer, Ph.D.,
Department of Literacy, College of Education,
Boise State University

COMPASS POINT BOOKS  MINNEAPOLIS, MINNESOTA

Compass Point Books
3109 West 50th Street, #115
Minneapolis, MN 55410

Visit Compass Point Books on the Internet at *www.compasspointbooks.com*
or e-mail your request to *custserv@compasspointbooks.com*

Editor: Heidi Schoof
Lead Designer: Jaime Martens
Photo Researcher: Svetlana Zhurkina
Page Production: Tom Openshaw
Cartographer: XNR Productions, Inc.
Educational Consultant: Diane Smolinski

Managing Editor: Catherine Neitge
Art Director: Keith Griffin
Production Director: Keith McCormick
Creative Director: Terri Foley

Library of Congress Cataloging-in-Publication Data
Burgan, Michael.
  Samuel Adams : patriot and statesman/ by Michael Burgan.
    p. cm.—(Signature lives)
  Includes bibliographical references and index.
  ISBN 0-7565-0823-1 (hardcover)
  1. Adams, Samuel, 1722-1803—Juvenile literature. 2. Politicians—United
States—Biography—Juvenile literature. 3. Revolutionaries—United States—
Biography—Juvenile literature. 4. United States. Declaration of
Independence—Signers—Biography—Juvenile literature. 5. United States—
History—Revolution, 1775-1783—Biography—Juvenile literature. I. Title.
II. Series.
  E302.6.A2B87 2005
  973.3'13'092--dc22   2004019871

REVOLUTIONARY WAR ERA

The American Revolution created heroes—and traitors—who shaped the birth of a new nation: the United States of America. "Taxation without representation" was a serious problem for the American colonies during the late 1700s. Great Britain imposed harsh taxes and didn't give the colonists a voice in their own government. The colonists rebelled and declared their independence from Britain—the war was on.

Table of Contents

1 A WANTED MAN

༒

Spies walked the streets of Boston in April 1775, and the threat of war filled the air. For more than 10 years, residents of the Massachusetts capital had been protesting British policies that limited their freedoms. Now, patriots outside the city were gathering weapons and supplies. They were ready to fight to defend their rights.

British general Thomas Gage was military governor of the Massachusetts Colony, and his troops controlled Boston. But the rebel colonists, as they prepared for war, looked to Samuel Adams for leadership. Adams was not only a courageous patriot, he was also a great writer, and he used his writing skills to ask Americans all over the colonies to support the Massachusetts patriots. He declared

Samuel Adams has been called the father of the American Revolution.

that the patriots were ready "to draw their swords in the defense of their liberties." Adams explained that the colonists must work together to resist the unfair policies of their British rulers.

General Gage knew through his spies that the Americans were storing gunpowder in Concord, about 20 miles (32 kilometers) west of Boston. He also knew that Samuel Adams was staying in nearby Lexington while he attended patriot meetings in Concord. In mid-April, Gage received a letter from British leaders in London. They wanted the general to do whatever he had to do to prevent an American

Samuel Adams and John Hancock stayed here at the Hancock-Clarke House in Lexington, Massachusetts.

rebellion—and that included arresting Samuel Adams.

Through spies of his own, Adams already knew that he was a wanted man. London newspapers that reached Boston also spelled out what the British thought of Adams. The papers said the patriot leader would be hanged if he were caught. Adams's friends suggested that he hire a bodyguard, but he refused. Even though he was in

John Hancock (1737-1793) was an important Boston businessman who became a revolutionary leader when Great Britain forced higher taxes on the colonies. Hancock was the first person to sign the Declaration of Independence and the only person to sign it on July 4, 1776.

danger, Samuel Adams left Boston along with fellow patriot leader John Hancock. The two men remained in Lexington after their meetings in Concord had ended. At times, armed guards were seen solemnly walking the grounds of the house where they stayed, on the watch for enemies.

On the night of April 18, 1775, residents of Boston saw British troops stirring around them. The hated "redcoats" were preparing to march to Concord and seize the patriots' supplies. Many colonists assumed that the soldiers would arrest Adams and Hancock as well. Several patriot riders left Boston, carrying the message that the British were on their way to Lexington and Concord. Today, the best known of these riders is Paul

Paul Revere warned colonists that British soldiers were on their way to Lexington.

Revere. He blazed across the countryside on horseback to the house where Adams and Hancock were staying and gave them the news. A church bell soon cut through the quiet night, calling patriot soldiers to defend their town.

Hancock, too, wanted to prepare for battle, but Adams said no. The patriots would need them as leaders during the war—they should not risk their lives fighting. Instead, Adams suggested that he and Hancock leave Lexington. As daylight came, the two men rode off in a carriage to Woburn, their first stop on a trip out of the colony. Adams, it has been reported, turned to Hancock and said, "Oh, what a glorious morning is this!" Although he did not welcome bloodshed, Samuel Adams was eager to defend the rights of Americans. One historian later called the war for independence "Sam Adams's Revolution."

Paul Revere (1734-1818) served as an important messenger for the patriot cause. He delivered news on horseback between the cities of Boston and Philadelphia. A silversmith by trade, Revere also worked as a copper-plate engraver, creating illustrations for magazines and other publications. He even did some dentistry— cleaning people's teeth and making dentures.

The next summer, Adams eagerly signed the Declaration of Independence. This document marked the formal break between the American colonies and Great Britain. Samuel Adams realized that the only way Americans could defend their rights was to form a new nation. ℘

2 A YOUNG PATRIOT

ಀ

English settlers first came to the Boston area around 1630. One of these early colonists was Henry Adams, the great-great-grandfather of Samuel Adams. The descendents of Henry Adams split into two distinct groups. The "country" Adamses lived in Braintree (now Quincy), about eight miles (13 km) outside of Boston. The second president of the United States, John Adams traced his roots to this branch. The other side of the Adams family, the "city" branch, settled in Boston. It was there that Samuel Adams Jr. was born on September 27, 1722.

Boston was the capital and business center of Massachusetts Colony. At the start of the 18th century, it was the largest city in Great Britain's North American colonies. From Boston

Native Americans welcomed Puritans with a gift of fish on the Charles River, Massachusetts, in 1635.

harbor, ships filled with lumber, fish, and other goods sailed to ports in Great Britain and its colonies in the West Indies. Other vessels arrived, carrying manufactured products from Great Britain and goods such as tea and cloth from far-off lands.

The streets of Boston also bustled with economic activity. Skilled craftsmen and their helpers produced goods such as silver and pewter plates, fine clothes and shoes, and wooden barrels and wheels. Printers published pamphlets and books, while lawyers in their offices gave legal advice. In this buzz of making, buying, and selling, Samuel Adams Sr. was one of the most successful Boston merchants.

Adams was a maltster. He took barley and turned it into malt, one of the key ingredients in beer. He then brewed the beer. Adams also took sweet, thick molasses and turned it into rum, another alcoholic drink. Over time, Adams used the profits from his business to buy land and houses across the city.

Samuel Adams Sr. and his wife Mary had 12 children. Samuel Jr. was one of only three who reached adulthood. The other surviving Adams children were Samuel's older sister, Mary, and his younger brother, Joseph. Thanks to his father's success, young Samuel lived in one of the finest

houses in Boston. His father was one of the city's most respected citizens. In addition, the Adams family had close ties to another influential Boston family, the Mathers. Young Samuel's grandfather married Maria Mather after his first wife died. Maria's father, Increase, was the leading minister in Boston when religion played an important role in the daily life of many colonists.

Samuel Adams spent most of his life in and around Boston, Massachusetts.

In the 1700s, Puritan ministers preached from pulpits like this one in Boston's Old South Meeting House.

Like the Mathers, Samuel Sr. and Mary Adams were deeply religious. They raised their children in the Congregational Church, which was founded by the Puritans. Adams was a deacon, one of the leaders of the Congregational Church, and neighbors often called him "Deacon Adams." He and his wife made sure their children followed the family faith. Samuel Jr. knew the Lord's Prayer by the time he was 2 years old. He learned the alphabet while he and his mother read from the Bible. As he grew older, young Samuel continued to be influenced by his Puritan background.

The Puritans believed that God chose certain people to go to heaven. A person's actions, whether good or bad, could not affect this choice. No one knew who these "elect," or chosen people, were, but the Puritans said all people should behave as if they were the elect. They should follow the teachings of the Bible, work hard, and lead simple lives.

The Puritans believed that everyone in a community had a duty to follow the laws and try to improve the community's morals. The Puritans believed in virtue, or doing the right thing at all times. People should be virtuous without seeking some kind of personal reward or benefit. These ideas influenced the political views of Samuel Adams in his adult life.

As a boy, Samuel attended Boston Latin School. To enter school, Samuel had to prove he

Puritans built the first large English settlement in Boston. For many years in Massachusetts, only members of this church could vote in local elections. Congregationalist attitudes also shaped the early laws of the colony. A person who decided to skip a Sunday church service might end up in the stocks. These large, sturdy pieces of wood were clamped around a person's hands and feet so they could not move. Everyone was expected to act like a Congregationalist, even if they did not hold Puritan beliefs.

could read from the Bible. Thanks to his mother's early training, he had no trouble passing this test. During his classes, Samuel sat on a wooden bench with other boys his age. They studied Greek and Latin because all educated people were expected to read these ancient languages. Samuel also improved his reading and writing skills in English. In the only notebook that survived his childhood, Samuel wrote that learning was more important than acquiring riches.

On two afternoons each week and all day Sunday, Samuel did not have to attend school. Like most boys in colonial Massachusetts, Samuel probably helped his father during that time. When the work was done, the boys of Boston enjoyed swimming and fishing in the waters surrounding their city. In wintertime, Samuel and his friends most likely went sledding and ice skating.

Many male members of Samuel Adams's family attended Harvard. The female members of the family, like all colonial women, were not allowed to attend college. In fact, most women received little formal schooling outside the home.

At the age of 14, Samuel entered Harvard, a college in nearby Cambridge, Massachusetts, which had been founded by Puritans in 1636. Most boys of the era entered college at that age. Samuel lived in Cambridge while attending Harvard. He continued

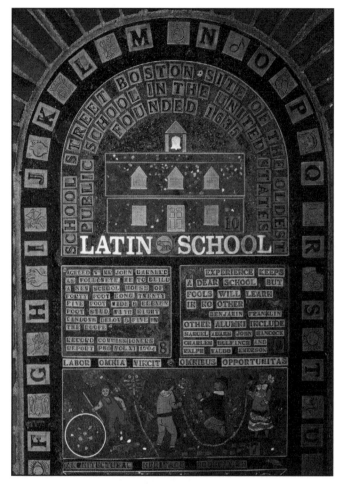

A unique mosaic marks the site of Boston Latin School, the oldest public school in the United States.

his study of ancient Greek and Roman writers. He also learned geography, religion, math, astronomy, and composition. A typical day for Samuel and his classmates began at 6 A.M. The students prayed together before eating breakfast and heading to class. Their work continued into the evening, when they were expected to study in their rooms.

Young men living away from home for the first time often like to test their new independence. For the boys of Harvard, one way to do this was to sneak off and drink alcohol. Some students even managed to brew beer in their rooms. On one occasion, Samuel and some classmates were fined for drinking. This must have been a disappointment to Samuel's Puritan parents. Even though his father was a brewer, the family was influenced by Puritan teachings to avoid drunkenness.

In 1740, Samuel graduated from Harvard. He considered becoming a minister and a lawyer

A view of Harvard College in Cambridge, Massachusetts, in 1739. The college gradually grew up around Harvard Yard, which remains the heart of the campus.

before finally deciding to study business. He earned his master's degree from Harvard in 1743.

Unfortunately, Samuel lacked his father's talent for making money. He did poorly working as a clerk in the counting house of Thomas Cushing, a family friend and one of the colony's leading merchants.

When his father loaned him money to start his own business, Samuel loaned most of it to a friend, who never paid him back. He lost the rest in his own business dealings. Thomas Cushing wrote that Adams had a sharp mind, "but he would never do for a merchant; his whole soul was engrossed in politics." ❧

3 AN INTEREST IN POLITICS

⤳⟨∝⟩⤶

All through his boyhood, Samuel had heard his father and his friends discussing the public affairs of Boston and the colony. Before Samuel was born, Adams Sr. won local elections. His political success added to his influence in the city. The elder Adams held a number of government positions, including justice of the peace, selectman, and representative to the General Court, the colony's governing body. The selectmen of Boston ran the town meeting, which was the local government.

Adams Sr. worked closely with a group of men known as the Boston Caucus. Meeting in clubs or taverns, the caucus members chose people to run for political office. They formed what was called the country party, or popular party. The members

The town meeting was the seat of local government in colonial America.

of the Boston Caucus usually supported the interests of Boston's working people. Their political opponents were called the court party. Its members usually supported the governor and other local officials who worked for the British. Samuel Adams shared his father's political beliefs and supported the popular party.

At Harvard, Samuel read the works of an English writer named John Locke. In 1690 Locke had published a book explaining his ideas on government. John Locke believed that God gave all humans natural rights. These included life, liberty,

John Locke (1632-1704) is known as the father of English empiricism, a theory that all knowledge comes from experience.

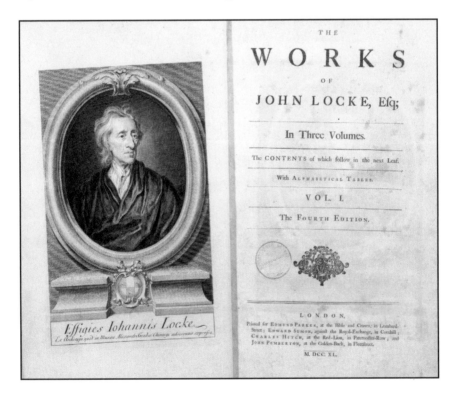

and the right to own property. No ruler could take away these rights. People also had a right, Locke said, "to resist the force of those who without authority would impose anything on them." Samuel Adams, like many future patriot leaders, embraced Locke's ideas. Adams combined these ideas with his father's devotion to protecting the interests of the common people.

In 1741, a political and economic crisis struck the Adams family. Samuel's father and some of his friends had started a bank that printed paper money backed by land. More than 800 people joined this so-called land bank. They borrowed money and promised to give their land to the bank if they could not repay the loan. Most of the borrowers were not wealthy.

Thomas Hutchinson was a leading member of Boston's court party who strongly opposed the operations of the land bank. He and other members of the court party believed that only gold or silver should be used as money. Together, they influenced the royal governor of Massachusetts, Jonathan Belcher, to shut down the bank. Adams Sr. and his partners lost a tremendous amount of money in the land bank crisis.

To make matters worse, Parliament passed a law saying that people who lost money when the bank closed could sue Adams and the other bank leaders. Samuel Adams spent more than 10 years trying to protect his family from losing money in these court cases. The land bank's failure and its results increased Samuel's desire to enter politics and weaken the court party's influence. The crisis also made lifelong political enemies of Samuel Adams and Thomas Hutchinson.

As a royal official, Hutchinson believed he was a servant of the king who had to obey all British laws, whether he agreed with them or not. Samuel Adams, on the other hand, believed it was his duty to resist unfair rule.

In 1746, 24-year-old Samuel Adams Jr. was elected to his first public office, as clerk of the Boston Market. The same year Adams entered politics, he and some friends started a political club. The club also published a newspaper. Adams probably wrote most of the articles, since the ideas in the paper matched what he said and wrote before the American Revolution. "The true object of loyalty," one article said, "is a good legal constitution, which … condemns every instance of

Thomas Hutchinson was appointed governor of Massachusetts in 1771. In a series of private letters, Hutchinson expressed his support for the use of British troops to put down rebellious forces in Boston. Samuel Adams later published these letters, and angry Massachusetts residents called for Hutchinson's resignation. Hutchinson went from being a respected member of the community to one of Massachusetts most hated villains.

oppression and lawless power."

At the time, Great Britain did not have a written constitution, as the United States does today. But Adams and others referred to the laws and customs that shaped the British government as a constitution. Adams believed that rulers could not violate the constitution. To him, a citizen's greatest duty was to protect the constitution and resist rulers who broke it.

Thomas Hutchinson (1711-1780)

In 1748, Samuel Adams Sr. died, and Adams Jr. took over the family's malting business. He struggled in that role, so he let his brother Joseph run some of their father's properties. Bored with business, Adams spent much of his free time with his father's friends, including the Reverend Richard Checkley. The Checkley and Adams families had been close for years. On October 1, 1749, Samuel married Elizabeth Checkley, the minister's daughter. They had known each other their whole lives. By all

There were many chores to be done in a colonial home. Everyone who was able helped with cooking, spinning, and churning the butter.

accounts, Samuel and Elizabeth had a loving marriage. He once praised Elizabeth's skill in running the household—not an easy task, given Samuel's difficulties with money.

The Adamses eventually had six children, though only two—Samuel and Hannah—reached adulthood. Their first child, a son named Samuel, was born on September 14, 1750, and died less than three weeks later. On October 16, 1751, Elizabeth gave birth to her second son, whom they also named Samuel. This Samuel lived to be an adult. Baby Joseph was born on June 23, 1753, and died the very next day. Mary was born exactly one year later on June 23, 1754, and lived to be 3 months old before dying on October 3, 1754. Baby Hannah, who also lived to adulthood, arrived on June 21, 1756. Her brother Samuel was then 4 years old.

In July 1757, Elizabeth gave birth to their sixth baby, a stillborn boy. The delivery left Mrs. Adams weak and sick, and she died a few weeks later. Her son, Samuel, was not yet 6; little Hannah was barely 1. Her husband, Samuel Adams, was crushed by the loss. But he found the strength to write glowing words of praise for Elizabeth: "To her husband she was as sincere a friend as she was faithful a wife." Adams hoped that his two surviving children would "inherit her graces!"

By the time of Elizabeth's death, Samuel Adams was one of Boston's tax collectors. He also became increasingly active in local politics.

Medical care was crude in colonial times, and people knew nothing about germs, so childbirth was risky for both mother and child. Infants often died of disease or were stillborn—already dead as they left their mothers' bodies. Many women died while giving birth to their children or soon afterwards, often from heavy bleeding or infection.

The popular party continued to hold closed meetings, called caucuses, as it had when Adams's father was alive. At the caucuses, party members selected political candidates and debated the party's position on key issues. The party then took the results of the caucuses to the town meeting. Adams played an active role in the caucuses, representing the city's workers and giving voice to their needs and concerns.

Adams was a natural politician. He got along with people from all backgrounds, and he spoke forcefully about the issues. He often spent his free time talking with sailors, craftsmen, and other workers in the city.

Samuel Adams worked for the interests of the working class.

But Adams's desire to get along with others hurt his business as tax collector. He sometimes let people go a long time without paying their taxes. By 1764 Adams had not collected all the taxes people owed. In fact, his accounts were very short of money. Some members of the court party criticized him for this. But by this time Samuel Adams was so widely known and so well-liked that the voters of Boston reelected him to another term.

According to his cousin John Adams, Samuel had "an exquisite ear for music and a charming voice." John also called him "a simple, decent citizen." Samuel Adams took pride in living simply and not trying to acquire a vast fortune—a sign of his family's Puritan background. Later in life, Adams said, "I glory in being what the world calls a poor man."

John Adams (1735-1826) was also an important figure during the American Revolution. John was Samuel's second cousin, and one of America's greatest political thinkers. He later became the first vice president of the United States and the second president of the United States.

His goal was not to become a rich man, but to become a politician who made sure the rights of the people of Boston were protected.

4 PROTESTING TAXES

Chapter

❧⌥❧

In 1754, war broke out in North America between Great Britain and France. Each country wanted to control the land between the Mississippi River and the English colonies along the Atlantic Ocean. France already claimed parts of Canada, the Great Lakes, and the land along the Mississippi River. Together with their Native American allies, the French fought the American colonists and British soldiers. This became known as the French and Indian War.

By 1760, the British had defeated the French in North America. That year, George III became king of England. George III thought that Parliament unfairly limited the power of the king. He insisted that he and his advisers have more control over the government.

After the victory over France, the British Parliament wanted the American colonists to pay for the war and for the troops that were still stationed at forts along the frontier. British prime minister George Grenville suggested imposing new taxes on the Americans to pay for these services. As prime minister, Grenville was the most powerful member of Parliament. King George III supported Grenville's effort to tax the colonies and tighten British control over them.

Americans already had to pay taxes called duties on certain goods brought into the colonies. Under the Molasses Act of 1733, merchants were required to pay a tax on any molasses that was brought in from another country. This law was rarely enforced, however, and many Americans avoided these duties by smuggling.

In 1764, Grenville proposed a law called the American Revenue Act, also known as the Sugar Act. This law lowered the tax on molasses, but placed new duties on other forms of sugar and items such as coffee, wine, textiles, and dye. The worst part was that Grenville had plans to make sure the new law would be strictly enforced.

The goal of the Sugar Act was to help pay the "expenses of defending, protecting, and securing the [American] colonies." To Samuel Adams and other Americans, this meant the Sugar Act was a tax, not a duty. Taxes were meant to raise money for government operations, while a duty was designed to promote or limit trade.

Parliament had ignored the usual process for passing tax laws. According to British legal customs, taxpayers had to approve new taxes through their elected representatives. Americans did not

George Grenville (1753-1813)

elect members of Parliament as British residents did. American interests were not represented in Parliament. Angry Americans such as Adams said there should be "no taxation without representation."

On May 24, 1764, the Boston Town Meeting approved a statement that Adams wrote to protest the Sugar Act—his first known public statement on British policies in the colonies. The act, he argued, destroyed "our ... right to govern and tax ourselves. It strikes at our British privileges, which ... we hold in common with our fellow-subjects who are natives of Britain."

The American colonies were not represented in Great Britain's House of Commons.

Boston was the first American city to claim that Parliament had violated the British constitution. Some merchants in other colonial cities joined the protest against the Sugar Act. Most Americans, however, did not speak out against it. They did not see the difference between the new duties and old duties. When the next tax was placed on the colonists, however, more and more Americans joined Adams in his protest.

In 1764, Samuel Adams married Elizabeth Wells, the daughter of a Boston merchant. Adams was now

42, while his new bride was 28. Betsy, as Adams called her, was a good mother to his children—Samuel, now 13, and Hannah, 8—and a devoted wife. Like Adams's first wife, Betsy was left to manage the household while her husband pursued his political interests. Samuel had never been particularly concerned with his appearance and was rather absentminded. At times, Betsy might have felt that she had a third child to care for.

At home with his family, Adams was a loving husband and father, even if his career kept him busy. Adams raised his two children in the Congregational Church and continued to attend services throughout his life.

His political enemies, such as Thomas Hutchinson, claimed Adams was a fake—that his religious "devotion" was a trick to win support from true Christians. But in his writings and actions, Adams often showed the virtue and honesty the early Puritans preached. To Adams, virtue meant giving up personal gain or pleasure to do what was right for the community. And only a "virtuous people" he once wrote "both deserve and enjoy" liberty.

Adams had been remarried for only several months when the next political bombshell hit the colonies. Early in 1765, Parliament passed the Stamp Act. It required Americans to pay a tax on paper products such as newspapers, business and

Lawyer James Otis Jr. argued against the use of writs, legal documents that allowed British officials to search private property for illegal goods.

legal documents, and playing cards. Government officials placed a stamp on the paper once the tax was paid.

Once again, Adams led the protests against the new tax. He called it unconstitutional. He added that even if the colonies could send representatives to Parliament, their interests would never be truly heard. The colonies were too far away from Great Britain to work closely with their representatives. Since telephones and telegraph machines had not yet been invented, all messages had to travel by ship. A voyage across the Atlantic could take months. By the time the colonists learned about a proposed law, Parliament would have already acted on it.

The Stamp Act was supposed to take effect on November 1, 1765. In Boston, Adams suggested that all the American colonies should work together to oppose the new tax. Another popular party member, James Otis Jr., also supported this idea, and he and Adams partnered to fight the Stamp Act.

Otis was the speaker of the Massachusetts General Court—the government body that passed laws for the colony—where Adams had risen to the position of clerk.

In June 1765, the General Court asked all the colonies to send representatives to a meeting. In October, representatives from nine colonies met in New York at the Stamp Act Congress. Together, they prepared a written statement called the Declaration of Rights and Grievances, outlining why the colonies opposed the tax. The Stamp Act Congress marked the first time that the colonies worked together to protest British policies.

Adams thought the Americans could defeat the Stamp Act by showing Parliament how the new tax violated the British constitution. He also supported a boycott of English goods as a form of protest. Other members of the popular party, however,

James Otis Jr. (1725-1783) was a lawyer and the most famous member of Boston's popular party when the Sugar and Stamp Acts were passed. He was also one of the first people to speak out against taxation without representation. For several years, Otis and Samuel Adams worked together against British taxes. In 1769, however, Otis suffered a head injury that affected his ability to think clearly. He lost influence in Boston politics and did not play a role during the American Revolution. He died in 1783 after being struck by lightning.

wanted to take more direct action against the tax. A group called the Loyal Nine organized a mob to protest the Stamp Act. They also formed a secret patriotic society called the Sons of Liberty. Branches of the Sons of Liberty soon sprang up in other colonies to protest the tax.

On August 14, the Loyal Nine's angry crowd marched through the streets of Boston. Some of them shouted, "Liberty, property, and no stamps!" Some of the protesters destroyed the property of the local official who was supposed to collect the new tax. They even wanted to kill him. A few weeks later, another mob, not connected to the Loyal Nine, stormed the house of Thomas Hutchinson. By this time, Hutchinson was lieutenant governor of Massachusetts Colony. At his home, the protesters stole books, clothing, and furniture. Governor Francis Bernard later wrote that everything movable in the home was destroyed.

Adams approved the first protest. It was aimed at someone who was directly connected to the new tax, and it had been organized by leading popular party members. In regard to that protest, Adams said that on August 14, "the people shouted; and their shout was heard to the distant end of this continent." But the second protest, he believed, had gone too far. Adams did not support stealing from Hutchinson's home, and he thought the crowd

had been out of control. Adams wanted men like himself and Otis to lead the protests, and he feared the crowd's actions might weaken support for the popular party.

Americans who opposed the Stamp Act were

Angry colonists burned paper items bearing British stamps in protest of the Stamp Act of 1765.

called Whigs. The Americans who supported the British government and its right to tax were called Tories. The American Whigs had many allies in London. The boycott of English goods had spread to other colonies, which caused British merchants to lose money, and they feared losing even more if Parliament did not repeal the Stamp Act. The merchants used their influence with the lawmakers, and Parliament repealed the tax in March 1766. British lawmakers, however, claimed they had a legal right to introduce new taxes in the future.

With the repeal of the Stamp Act, Samuel Adams turned his attention to strengthening the popular party. He looked for talented men who supported the party's aims. In the Massachusetts General Court, Adams began to work with lawmakers from the countryside, expanding the influence of the Boston patriots outside the city. Meeting in smoky taverns and private clubs, Adams and other party leaders chose patriots to run for local government offices and then called on voters to back their choices. After the Stamp Act, Adams feared Parliament would try to deny American rights again. He wanted to make sure the popular party had enough power to challenge those efforts.

In 1767, a British official named Charles Townshend convinced Parliament to pass several laws that affected the American colonies. These laws were called the Townshend Acts. They included new duties on such items as tea, glass, and paper. Some patriots angrily attacked the Townshend Acts, and a few in Boston called for armed rebellion. Although not ready to battle the British, Adams once again used his pen in the cause of liberty. By now he was a leader in the Massachusetts House, one branch of the General Court.

British Chancellor of the Exchequer Charles Townshend

In January 1768 he helped write a letter to Great Britain's King George III. Adams explained why the colonists opposed the Townshend Acts and asked the king to help them. The Massachusetts colonists were still loyal to King George, Adams said. They did not want their independence. They simply wanted Parliament to respect their rights. The most important right, Adams wrote, was to be "taxed only by representatives of their own free election."

Adams constantly wrote articles and letters defending the Americans' constitutional rights. His

Samuel Adams spent a lot of time at his desk.

dedication to the cause amazed both his family and friends. Long after the American Revolution, Elizabeth Adams noted that she often heard the scratching of her husband's pen on paper late into the evening. Well past midnight, neighbor Joseph Pierce said, a single lamp burned in Adams's window, and Pierce knew that Sam Adams was hard at work writing against the Tories.

In the Massachusetts House, Adams and other leaders tried to get more colonies to join their protests. Adams wrote what was called a circular letter. It outlined the House's concerns about taxation without representation and was then sent around to the lawmakers in other colonies. As the Revolution approached, Adams wrote more circular letters to unite the colonies against the British. Adams and the Massachusetts House also called for another boycott of British goods. A few colonies followed Massachusetts's lead and agreed not to import British goods. 🐚

Chapter

5 THE CENTER OF REBELLION

❧❦❧

The Townshend Acts created new problems in Boston. Under the acts, Great Britain sent officials called customs commissioners to the city. Their job was to put an end to smuggling in the colonies. Boston residents did not like the commissioners, and the officials sensed this hatred. They asked British leaders to send a naval ship to Boston to protect them. The warship *Romney* reached the city in May 1768. Its presence angered many residents. British naval officers made things worse when they forced Americans to serve on the ship. Adams led a committee that protested this impressment and the presence of British military forces in the city.

In June 1768, the Bostonians' anger led to violence. The customs commissioners worked with

British soldiers and American colonists worked in the Boston harbor in the 1770s.

the captain of the *Romney* to seize a colonial ship, the *Liberty.* Its owner was John Hancock, a wealthy patriot merchant. Like many others, Hancock had ignored the duties he was supposed to pay on the cargo his ships carried. When British sailors arrived to board the *Liberty*, a mob began throwing rocks at them. Other protesters attacked the homes of the customs officials. Later, a spy told Thomas Hutchinson that Adams had called on Boston residents to take their weapons and attack British officials. Adams supposedly said that 30,000 men would join them from the country. The spy's claim, however, seems false, since Adams often condemned mob violence. He knew that destructive acts would turn some residents of Massachusetts against the patriots. Through powerful arguments, not blows, Adams believed he could win more support for the patriot cause.

The *Liberty* violence upset Governor Bernard. Local police could not keep order in the city, and

The British accused John Hancock of smuggling and dodging taxes.

Boston's patriot-controlled courts refused to punish the rioters. In Great Britain, government officials saw Boston as the heart of a growing problem. The British were convinced they had their own constitutional right to run their colonies as they pleased. British leaders decided they would assert their rights and end the protests in Boston. They decided to send troops to the city to enforce British rule and protect government officials.

The British troops that served in the American colonies were known as "lobsterbacks" or "redcoats" because of the long, red jackets they wore. Although the Americans had fought side-by-side with the redcoats during the French and Indian War, they did not respect each other. The regulars did not think much of the Americans' fighting skills. The Americans thought the British soldiers lacked morals and their officers were cruel.

In September 1768, Bostonians learned the British troops would soon appear. Samuel Adams quickly took action to protest their arrival. He called for a meeting of patriot officials from neighboring

The British regulars (meaning full-time professional soldiers) were not trained to aim when they shot. They marched in tight rows and simply fired straight ahead at the enemy. The redcoats preferred to get close to the enemy and use their bayonets. Because their guns weren't very accurate, using the bayonet was probably more effective than shooting.

towns. About 90 towns sent delegates to this convention. The meeting, however, did not stir the strong anti-British feelings Adams wanted. The thought that troops would soon be in Boston seemed to weaken some patriots' desire to resist.

The redcoats began arriving on October 1, 1768. Many of them slept in barracks at Castle William, an island in Boston harbor. During the day, however, the soldiers trained in the city and patrolled the streets. Adams was angry when the soldiers stopped residents and asked where they were going. "To be called to account by a common soldier," he wrote, "is a badge of slavery."

Adams supposedly trained Queue, his faithful Newfoundland dog, to snarl and snap at the British soldiers when they passed by. Years after the American Revolution, John Adams recalled how his cousin Samuel had trained John's son, John Quincy Adams, to despise the British troops, and admire the Boston militia.

Over time, British soldiers and Boston residents sometimes traded insults or started fistfights. The bad feelings finally led to a bloody clash known as the Boston Massacre. The troubles began on March 2, 1770. A British soldier got into an argument with the owner of a ropewalk, where ropes were made, and his workers. Soon a riot started between British soldiers and the workers. Over the

next several days, both sides waited for a chance to renew the fight.

On the night of March 5, a crowd began insulting and throwing snowballs at a guard outside the customs house. When more British troops came to help him, they fired into the crowd, killing five Americans. The local patriots called the killings the Boston Massacre. They hoped to stir up anti-British feelings and increase support for the patriot cause.

The next day, Adams used the massacre as an

British soldiers fired on a crowd of colonists. This attack was later called the Boston Massacre.

Samuel Adams warned Thomas Hutchinson after the Boston Massacre.

argument for sending all the British troops out of the city to Castle William, in Boston harbor. Thomas Hutchinson was the acting governor at that time. At first he refused to move the troops. Adams then led a public meeting where he spoke with deep passion. Adams blamed Hutchinson for not using his legal power to send the troops out of the city. The people voted to ask Hutchinson again, so Adams led a small committee to meet with the governor.

Hutchinson later wrote that Adams showed "a strong expression of that determined spirit" for which he would become famous. Adams said, "The meeting is composed of three thousand people.

They are become very impatient. A thousand men are already arrived from the neighborhood, and the country is in general motion."

Adams warned that if more blood were spilled, it would be Hutchinson's fault. With this threat of more violence, the governor gave in and agreed to send the troops to Castle William. Some British officials began calling the troops "Samuel Adams's Regiments," because Adams had used his political skill to force their removal. With the removal of the troops, the city became calm again.

Because of the massacre, eight British soldiers and one officer were accused of murder and put on trial. Samuel's cousin John Adams served as their lawyer. In the end, John Adams convinced the jury that six of the eight soldiers had fired their guns in self-defense. They were found innocent. Two other soldiers were found guilty of the lesser crime of manslaughter.

After the trial, Samuel Adams wrote many articles about the massacre. He questioned British policies in America, and accused British leaders of trying to "enslave and ruin the colonies."

Samuel Adams and other patriot leaders asked John Adams to defend the soldiers. Samuel did not want the actions of the mob that led to the massacre to weaken the patriot cause. He feared that local residents would think the patriot leaders had ordered the mob to riot. Samuel knew that John Adams would argue that the mob acted on its own.

By the time of the Boston Massacre, Samuel Adams was once again struggling to pay his bills. In 1764, Adams had closed the family brewery because he could not afford to make repairs or pay his workers. Adams received a small salary for his work in the Massachusetts General Court, and he also had income from the family wharf. Some people have claimed that his friend John Hancock secretly slipped Adams money to pay his bills.

In April 1771, Samuel Adams lost an election for a local office in Suffolk County, where Boston was located. But Adams still had his seat in the Massachusetts House, and he was considered the leader of the patriots there. He worked hard to stir up more support for the patriot cause in Massachusetts and across the colonies. In one article Adams wrote, "It is by united councils ... that this continent must expect to recover its violated rights and liberties."

To achieve this unity, Adams proposed forming a Committee of Correspondence. This committee would discuss local political concerns and share ideas with similar committees throughout Massachusetts Colony. Thomas Hutchinson called the idea "a foolish scheme." But patriot lawmakers in the colony liked the idea.

Boston's Committee of Correspondence formed in 1772, and within a year, Massachusetts had 80

BOSTON, September, 27, 1774.

GENTLEMEN,

THE committees of correspondence of this and several of the neighbouring towns, having taken into consideration the vast importance of withholding from the troops now here, labour, straw, timber, flitwork, boards, and in short every article excepting provisions necessary for their subsistance; and being under a necessity from their conduct of considering them as real enemies, we are fully satisfied that it is our bounden duty to withhold from them every thing but what meer humanity requires; and therefore we must beg your close and serious attention to the inclosed resolves which were passed unanimously; and as unanimity in all our measures in this day of severe trial, is of the utmost consequence, we do earnestly recommend your co-operation in this measure, as conducive to the good of the whole.

We are,

Your Friends and Fellow Countrymen,

Signed by Order of the joint Committee,

William Cooper Clerk.

such committees. Other colonies formed committees as well, and Adams suggested the committees from each colony should share ideas with each other. Virginia lawmakers agreed, and they asked other colonies to join this new system of political action.

In Massachusetts, Thomas Hutchinson was now officially governor. He tried to weaken the patriots in the General Court whenever he could. At times, he refused to let the General Court meet at all because he feared Adams and other patriots would

Committees of correspondence shared ideas and helped to unite the colonies in political action.

challenge him. Yet with the committees of correspondence in place, the patriot lawmakers could still meet and plan their actions against the British.

In Boston, the Adams home became a popular spot for political gatherings. Patriots from Massachusetts and other colonies often stayed there, with Elizabeth somehow finding a way to keep the guests fed and comfortable. John Adams noted that his cousin was "ambitious of entertaining his friends handsomely," even as he "affects to despise riches." Meanwhile, spies took note of all who met with Adams and passed the information to Governor Hutchinson.

In 1770, Parliament had canceled all the duties from the Townshend Acts, except the tax on imported tea. Americans loved tea, but many had pledged not to drink it to protest the tax. Others avoided the tax by smuggling tea into the colonies.

The largest conflict over the tea came in Boston. On December 16, 1773, more than 5,000 people crammed into the Old South Meeting House. Dock workers were to begin unloading tea the next morning from a British ship in the harbor. Two more ships would unload their cargo of tea in the days ahead. The crowd was determined to stop them.

Samuel Adams and other leading patriots had asked Governor Hutchinson to send the tea ships back to Great Britain. Hutchinson refused, and he ordered British admiral John Montague to stop any

*Old South
Meeting House
in Boston*

ship that tried to sneak out of the harbor. The patriots also asked Francis Rotch, the owner of one of the
tea ships, to send his ship out of the harbor without
unloading the tea. Rotch said no, unless Hutchinson
approved. On December 16, Rotch visited Hutchinson, asking him once more to let the tea ship leave.
Hutchinson once again denied the request.

Around 6:00 P.M. Rotch entered the Old South

Meeting House, which was jammed with people. The crowd stirred with anger as Rotch reported that the duty had to be paid before his ship could leave. Otherwise, the tea would be unloaded the next morning. The crowd finally quieted as Samuel Adams rose to speak. "This meeting," he said, "can do nothing more to save the country." Many historians think this line was a signal for others to take action.

As Adams finished speaking, some people in the crowd began to shout. "Boston Harbor a teapot tonight!" yelled one. Another cried, "The Mohawks are come!" Sure enough, a group of men dressed as Mohawk Indians appeared in the doorway. They wore black paint or soot on their skin and had wrapped blankets around their bodies. The "Mohawks" wanted to hide their true identities. They were actually Boston patriots ready to protest the tax on tea.

Adams knew about the "Mohawks" and their plan. He and other patriot leaders had met secretly before the December 16 public meeting. They decided to take forceful action if Hutchinson would not let the tea ships leave the harbor. Now, the "Mohawks" and a large crowd approached the docks. The raiders boarded the three ships and dumped 342 crates of tea into the water.

The patriots who boarded the tea ships worked silently and were careful not to damage the ships

or hurt anyone on board. They used tomahawks to split open the tea chests before throwing them into the water. After about three hours, the rebels were done. This late-night raid is now known as the Boston Tea Party.

A few weeks later, Adams sent a letter to a friend about the protest. He wrote, "You cannot imagine the height of joy that sparkles in the eyes … of all we meet on this occasion."

George Hewes was one of the "Mohawks" who took part in the Boston Tea Party. Years later, he described the scene of the next morning:

Patriots disguised as Mohawk Indians carried out the late-night raid known as the Boston Tea Party.

" ... after we had cleared the ships of the tea, it was discovered that very considerable quantities of it were floating upon the surface of the water; and to prevent the possibility of any of its being saved for use, a number of small boats were manned by sailors and citizens, who rowed them into those parts of the harbor wherever the tea was visible, and by beating it with oars and paddles so thoroughly drenched it as to render its entire destruction inevitable."

Bostonians had led the fight against taxes for several years, and the British did not welcome this interference. Parliament immediately punished the city of Boston for its latest protest. British lawmakers shut down the city's harbor and limited the powers of the local governments in Massachusetts. King George ordered that a military governor take control of the colony. The residents of Boston called these actions the Intolerable Acts.

By the spring of 1774, the committees of correspondence and the Sons of Liberty across the colonies had swung into action. Patriots held rallies to support Massachusetts and condemn the Intolerable Acts. Some colonies sent food to Massachusetts since ships could no longer bring supplies to Boston. One committee of correspondence in New Hampshire sent money. The people felt it was their duty to help, as the residents of

Massachusetts were "defending the common interests of a whole continent and gloriously struggling in the cause of liberty."

An advertisement of the Sons of Liberty requesting a meeting

In New York and Virginia, lawmakers said all the colonies should meet to discuss what the British were doing in Massachusetts. The colonists called this meeting the Continental Congress. Massachusetts chose Samuel Adams as one of its representatives. His goal of uniting all Americans against the British was being realized. Now he would have a chance to share his political ideas with some of the greatest leaders in the colonies. ℘

6 THE ROAD TO WAR

Chapter

©×©

At 52 years old, Samuel Adams prepared for his first trip outside of Massachusetts. His health was a concern, as he sometimes showed signs of palsy. But his mind was as sharp as ever, and his passion for protecting American rights never weakened.

Before Adams left for Philadelphia, his neighbors donated new clothes for him to wear at the congress. They knew he had few good clothes and could not afford to buy any on his own. Neighbors also helped repair his house and replace an old barn that was almost ready to collapse. Adams had continued to live simply, and he avoided the fashions that most men wore. Politics, always, was his main concern.

Adams traveled to Philadelphia with his cousin John and two other delegates. They journeyed in a

The First Continental Congress met at Carpenters' Hall in Philadelphia.

horse-drawn carriage across Massachusetts and through Connecticut, New York, and New Jersey. In some towns, hundreds of patriots came out to greet them. Samuel Adams was the true hero of the group. The people realized he had taken the major role in defending the colonists' constitutional rights.

The congress Adams attended in September 1774 is known today as the First Continental Congress. A second congress was held in the spring of 1775.

The First Continental Congress opened on September 5, 1774. Every colony except Georgia sent delegates to the meeting. Adams sometimes sent news about the congress to the Boston Committee of Correspondence. In one early letter, he wrote that the delegates "seem fully sensible of the intolerable grievances which the colonies are struggling under." Still, the delegates did not always agree about the problems with Great Britain and what to do about them.

Adams led a group of delegates who wanted to

John Adams served two terms as vice president under George Washington before he became the second president of the United States.

make a strong statement against British policies. Others joining him included Patrick Henry of Virginia. Henry said that since British troops now ruled in Boston, "all government is at an end," and the colonies were no longer separate. "I am not a Virginian," he said, "but an American."

Samuel Adams had similar thoughts, but his cousin John believed he should not say much about them. John knew that many of the delegates did not want to talk about anything that hinted at rebellion or independence. Even in Massachusetts, many colonists still believed they could repair their relations with Parliament and remain part of Great Britain. The key issue was getting the British to admit they had violated the constitution and to restore the colonists' rights.

After more than a month of debate, the First Continental Congress approved a set of resolutions. Many of the resolutions reflected what Adams had been saying and writing for years: Americans were entitled to life, liberty, and property, and they would not let anyone take those things away without their

> *Whenever his political career took him away from home, Adams exchanged letters with his wife, Betsy. She shared his political views and supported his efforts against the British. In one of her letters to Adams in Philadelphia in 1774, Betsy insulted Thomas Hutchinson and complained that the Tories had made Boston "a den of thieves, a cage of every unclean bird."*

> THE
>
> # PETITION
>
> OF THE
>
> GRAND AMERICAN CONTINENTAL
>
> # CONGRESS,
>
> TO THE
>
> # K I N G's
>
> Moſt Excellent Majeſty.
>
> ━━━━━━━━━━━━━
>
> A M E R I C A:
>
> Boſton, Printed and ſold at the Printing-Office, near
> the Mill-Bridge.

consent. Parliament, the resolutions said, had no right to create any laws that affected the colonies, except regarding trade.

The Congress also called for a boycott of British goods in every colony. By the next year, the colonies would also stop selling goods to Great Britain. Local residents in every town were supposed to write down the names of people who ignored these policies. The names would then be published, so patriots could break off all dealings with them. Adams approved of the results of the congress. He was glad to see that the colonies were working together to preserve their rights.

When he returned to Massachusetts in November, Adams served in a new government the colonists had created. Under British law, this government was illegal, but General Thomas Gage, the military governor of Massachusetts, did not shut it down. He also did not arrest Adams, which he had the power to do at any time. Gage knew either action might spark more violence, which he wanted to avoid. The Massachusetts patriots, however, believed war was coming soon. They gathered guns and supplies and trained the militia to prepare for war.

As war seemed more likely, Adams searched for possible allies. He hoped the Americans would receive aid from Canada, which was also a British colony. In February 1775, the Boston Committee of Correspondence sent a letter to local officials in Montreal and Quebec City explaining that British policies threatened their rights, too. He said that the Canadians would greatly help the common cause if they sent delegates to the next Continental Congress. The Canadians, however, did not join the effort.

Adams also tried to form an alliance with certain Native American tribes against the British. He led a committee that talked to the Mohawks, one of the Iroquois tribes of New York. At the least, Adams hoped the Mohawks would not join the British against the Americans. These efforts, however, failed. When the Revolutionary War began, the Iroquois fought for the British.

Samuel Adams failed in his attempts to form alliances with Canadians and Native Americans against the British.

The resolutions of the Continental Congress angered Parliament and King George III. The king saw that Massachusetts was rebelling against his power and the other colonies were ready to help it. In November 1774, King George wrote in a letter to his aide that "blows must decide whether they [the colonists] are to be subject to this country or independent." The king was ready to use military force to regain control.

Thanks to an American spy, General Gage knew about the patriots' military preparations. By April 1775, he decided to act. He sent about 700 redcoats to march from Boston to Concord, about 20 miles (32 km) west of the city. The troops would seize the gunpowder and weapons the Americans had stored there.

The British troops began their mission on the night of April 18. Samuel Adams and John Hancock were hiding in Lexington at the time, for fear that the British might arrest them if they stayed in Boston. As the British troops left the city, Paul Revere and William Dawes rode to warn Adams in Lexington and the people in Concord that the British were on their way.

Revere reached Adams and Hancock at about midnight. Early the next morning, the two patriot leaders left Lexington and headed to a nearby town for safety. From there they would travel on to Philadelphia for the Second Continental Congress.

Colonial Minutemen fought the redcoats on Lexington Common.

Meanwhile, in Lexington, fighting broke out between the colonists and the redcoats. No one is sure who fired first, but eight Americans were killed. The British then marched on to Concord, where they failed to find the patriots' supplies. The residents had already moved the gunpowder out of town and hidden the weapons and food. Finally, the local militias approached the British troops at a bridge. Both sides fired, and the battle was later called "the shot heard round the world." The Revolutionary War had begun.

The American soldiers who fought at Lexington and Concord included members of a special force called the Minutemen. These soldiers were chosen from the ranks of the local militias. Minutemen were always ready to march or fight at a minute's notice.

In June, General Gage said he would not arrest American rebels and their supporters if they stopped fighting. The offer applied to all patriots—except John Hancock and Samuel Adams. Gage said that their actions could not be forgiven and they had to stand trial for defying King George. He even offered a reward for their capture. To the British, Adams was a dangerous criminal. To patriots, he was the man who had helped spark a revolution for their rights.

Adams hoped the war would lead to complete independence from Great Britain. Few Americans had openly talked about breaking away from Great Britain to form their own country. Adams, however, believed independence was the only path Americans could follow to protect their rights forever. ❧

> *The town of Worcester, Massachusetts, recruited the first Minutemen in September 1774, and other towns in the colony soon followed it. Minutemen elected their own officers and trained several days a week. After the battles at Lexington and Concord, most Minutemen joined the Continental Army, the national military force commanded by General George Washington.*

7 INDEPENDENCE

Chapter

⎯⎯⎯ ❧❧❧ ⎯⎯⎯

Adams and Hancock reached Philadelphia in early May 1775. Adams now saw no hope for the colonies to remain part of Great Britain. Although most of the other delegates did not share Adams's desire for independence, to King George III all the members of Congress were traitors. Under British law, they could have been executed for rebelling against the king. Despite this, the other colonies were ready to join Massachusetts in its war against Great Britain. John Adams suggested that George Washington should lead a new Continental Army, and Congress agreed.

Even before reaching Philadelphia, Samuel Adams was thinking of ways to fight the British. On the trip there in April 1775, Adams and Hancock stopped in Hartford, Connecticut. They held a secret meeting with Jonathan Trumbull, the colony's patriot governor. Adams described his fear that the British would attack New England from Fort Ticonderoga, New York. He urged Connecticut's patriot leaders to raise a force and attack the fort first.

Governor Trumbull then recruited Ethan Allen, a Connecticut native who had moved to what is now Vermont. Another Connecticut native, Benedict Arnold, also joined Allen and his men. (Later in the war, Arnold became a traitor and fought for the British.) In May, Arnold, Allen, and a militia known as the Green Mountain Boys won the first major American victory of the Revolution. They took Fort Ticonderoga and captured cannons used against the British later in the war.

In Philadelphia, Samuel Adams learned some bad news from home. His best friend, Dr. Joseph Warren, had died fighting the British. The war had continued in and around Boston since the battles of April 19. Adams worried that the fighting could harm his family as well. He wrote to Betsy, "My great concern is for your health and safety."

Adams was also worried about his son. Now a doctor, the younger Samuel Adams had been captured by the British. Adams was relieved to hear a few weeks later that his son had managed to escape. The elder Adams then arranged for young Samuel to serve as a military surgeon for the patriots.

Ethan Allen and the Green Mountain Boys captured Fort Ticonderoga, New York.

As the war developed, Adams had a keen interest in military affairs and the need for a strong army. When the congress approved building 13 naval ships, Adams said it should build at least twice as many. He served on a committee in charge of supplying the troops, and he studied what the individual colonies could do to defend themselves. Thomas Jefferson later wrote that Adams had done more than any other representative to shape the war effort in the northern colonies.

By early 1776, fighting between the Americans and the British had spread to other colonies. That June, the Second Continental Congress began to

*Major battles
of the
Revolution
were fought
throughout
the colonies.*

debate whether the colonies should declare their
independence. Some leaders still hoped Americans
could both protect their rights and remain loyal
British citizens. Adams, along with his cousin

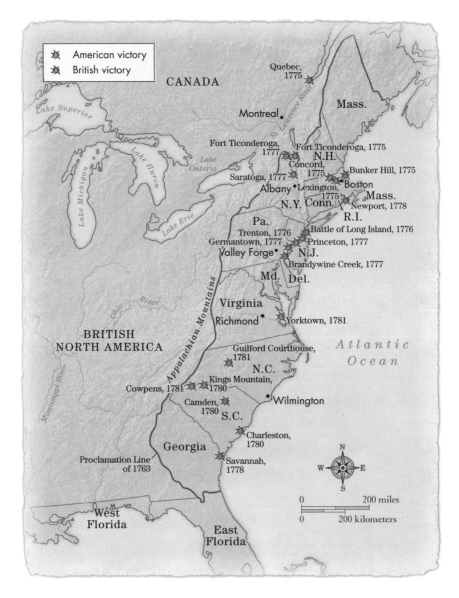

American victory
British victory

CANADA

Quebec, 1775

Mass.

Lake Superior

Montreal

St. Lawrence River

Lake Huron

Lake Michigan

Lake Ontario

Lake Erie

Fort Ticonderoga, 1777

Fort Ticonderoga, 1775

N.H.

Concord, 1775

Saratoga, 1777

Bunker Hill, 1775

Albany

Lexington, 1775

Boston

Mass.

N.Y.

Conn.

Newport, 1778

R.I.

Pa.

Battle of Long Island, 1776

Trenton, 1776

Germantown, 1777

Princeton, 1777

Valley Forge

N.J.

Brandywine Creek, 1777

Ohio River

Appalachian Mountains

Md.

Del.

Virginia

Richmond

Yorktown, 1781

Mississippi River

BRITISH
NORTH AMERICA

Atlantic
Ocean

Guilford Courthouse, 1781

N.C.

Cowpens, 1781

Kings Mountain, 1780

Camden, 1780

Wilmington

S.C.

Georgia

Charleston, 1780

Proclamation Line
of 1763

Savannah, 1778

N
W   E
S

0   200 miles
0   200 kilometers

West
Florida

East
Florida

John Adams and several other patriots, argued for independence.

Some of the delegates distrusted Samuel Adams. He seemed to work behind the scenes, trying to sway members' opinions, rather than debating ideas in the open. But Adams knew that personal contact and persuasion were his greatest strengths. He worked non-stop to convince the other delegates to support independence. Joseph Galloway, a delegate from Pennsylvania, wrote that Adams "eats little, drinks little, sleeps little, thinks much, and is most decisive … in the pursuit of his objects."

Most of what the delegates said at the congress is unknown because debates were held in secret and were not written down. Even in private, Adams preferred not to put his thoughts into writing, in case political enemies found out his plans. In his Philadelphia hotel room, Adams cut up the letters he received and tossed the tiny bits out the window, "to be scattered by the winds," as John Adams noted. Samuel disposed of early drafts of his own writings in the same way.

On July 1, 1776, the Second Continental Congress met to debate the Declaration of Independence, which was written mostly by Thomas Jefferson. The delegates sweltered through the summer heat as they argued one last time whether the American colonies should break away from Great Britain.

Finally, on July 4, 1776, the delegates approved

John Hancock boldly signed the Declaration of Independence large enough for King George to read "without his spectacles."

the Declaration of Independence, creating the United States of America. A relieved Adams told a friend he wished the declaration had come months before, but he knew he could not worry about the past. He wrote, "Let us do better for the future."

In August, Adams gave a speech praising America's independence. He had not talked much about religion during his political career. Now, however, he said "the hand of Heaven" had guided the Americans to take this bold step. He told his listeners, "Our union is now complete ... You are now the guardians of your own liberties."

One thing, however, was not complete. The United States of America needed its own government. Members of the Second Continental Congress began debating what form that government should take. Adams served on the committee that helped create the Articles of Confederation.

The Articles were a written constitution that spelled out the relationship between the states. Together, the states formed a "league of friendship," yet each state controlled its own affairs. Congress would have limited powers as the governing body over all the states. Adams supported the Articles of Confederation and asked the lawmakers in Massachusetts to accept it "for the sake of that Union which is so necessary for the support of the great cause."

In 1779, Adams returned to Boston to help create the state's first constitution. By this time, Adams's old friend John Hancock had become his political enemy. Adams thought Hancock now favored the rich over the average citizens. He feared Hancock and his allies might weaken the rights of Massachusetts voters. He fought to make sure they did not.

The General Court had drafted a constitution in 1778. Massachusetts voters, however, rejected it because it did not have a bill of rights. Some states had already

Adams returned home to Massachusetts a few times while he served in the Second Continental Congress. On one trip home, he rode on horseback—something he had not done for many years. He considered the 300-mile (480-km) ride a healthy exercise.

81

adopted a bill of rights, which protected specific personal rights and freedoms. These usually included the right to free speech, to belong to any religion, and to receive a trial by jury. In May 1779, the General Court called for a convention to create another constitution. Boston chose Adams as one of its delegates to this convention.

Adams and his cousin John served on the committee that wrote the Massachusetts Constitution. John Adams was the actual author, but Samuel influenced the debate that shaped the final document. The constitution was finished early in 1780. It included a Declaration of Rights, which was similar to a bill of rights. Many of the rights reflected Adams's usual ideas on government. The constitution said, "The people of this commonwealth have the

The Constitution of the commonwealth of Massachusetts

sole and exclusive right of governing themselves" and "all power resid[es] originally in the people." Yet Adams also supported limits on elections. Like most political leaders of that time, he thought only men who owned property or had a certain amount of wealth should vote.

Massachusetts voters approved the new constitution, and in September they prepared for their first election under it. Adams hoped the voters would elect wise leaders who would work for the good of the commonwealth. He was disappointed when the voters chose John Hancock as their first governor. He feared his old friend might try to rule like a king. But if he did, Adams had faith that the voters would not choose Hancock again during the next election.

Samuel Adams served in the Continental Congress until April 1781. In October, after Adams had returned to Boston, the Continental Army won a major victory at Yorktown. Not long afterwards, the British government decided to stop fighting and accept American independence. When the peace treaty was finally signed in 1783, Samuel Adams's dream for the United Staes of America became a reality. ❧

8 LAST YEARS

Chapter

❧❀❧

When Adams returned to Boston, he and Betsy moved into a rented house. The old family mansion had been damaged during the war, and most of the family's belongings had been stolen or destroyed by the British.

Although many patriot leaders made money during the war by selling and shipping supplies, Adams came home a poor man. He was relieved when his daughter, Hannah, married Captain Thomas Wells, "a gentleman who could at least raise her above the poverty to which she had so often been subjected."

During the war, Adams had been the Massachusetts secretary of state. In 1780, however, voters chose a man named John Avery to fill that

The Old State House in Boston was painted by James B. Marston in 1801.

Samuel Adams also
found time for city
politics. At the end of
1781, Adams was asked
to lead a committee to
study public education
in Boston. Adams
called for better school-
ing for the poor and
for young girls. At the
time, most girls did not
go to school. He had
instructed his own
daughter Hannah
during her younger
years, when he was not
too busy with political
affairs. Adams
believed that all
Americans had a right
to a good education.

position. Some of Samuel's friends suggested that John Hancock had worked against him during the election, but Adams accepted his defeat without complaining. While still in Philadelphia, he wrote to Betsy saying that the voters had the right to choose whomever they pleased, and that a defeated official should "cheer-fully" leave office. But his political career was not yet over.

Adams was still a powerful writer, and he wrote several articles leading up to the 1781 state elec-tions. Adams continued to believe that John Hancock was a bad choice for governor, and he worked for Hancock's defeat. Still, the governor easily won reelection. That same year, Adams was elected to the Massachusetts State Senate. He held that office until 1788.

Although the United States had won its inde-pendence, the new nation faced several challenges. Congress was the only branch of the new gov-ernment. There was no president or national court system as we have today. Adams called

Congress "the cement of the union" of the states. Some Americans, however, began to complain that Congress was too weak. The United States owed money to foreign bankers, but the states resisted paying taxes. Congress could pass laws, but it could not force the states to follow them. The government also lacked a good system for dealing with other nations. Some U.S. leaders began to suggest that the national government should be changed to give it more powers.

Young girls would eventually join boys in school

An angry mob seized a Massachusetts courthouse during Shays' Rebellion.

An incident in Massachusetts added to the concerns about the new government. In 1786, a group of farmers led by Daniel Shays protested new taxes and other state policies that they believed weakened their political rights. Adams did not support Shays' Rebellion, as the protest was called. After all, Massachusetts voters had elected representatives who approved the taxes. Adams wrote a letter that called for the protesters to stop their violence and accept the laws. Instead, the farmers tried to take some guns held in a U.S. government building. State troops stopped them, and four people were killed.

Although Massachusetts was able to end the rebellion, some Americans feared larger protests could erupt. If they did, the U.S. government was not strong enough to stop them. The protests also reflected confusion in the country over taxes and the money system. Some states allowed the use of old paper money that had no real value.

Shays' Rebellion convinced many leaders that the Articles of Confederation had to be changed. In 1787, leaders from each state except Rhode Island met in Philadelphia. At this convention, they created the U.S. Constitution that exists today. The Constitution gave the national government more powers while still protecting the rights of state governments. This system is sometimes called a federal system, and the national government is called the federal government.

At first Adams opposed the Constitution and the new government it created. He disliked having a strong national government that was separate from the states and had great power over them. Adams doubted that the new Congress could pass laws that would satisfy the different interests of all the citizens in such a large country. He also believed the

By the 1790s, two political parties had formed in the United States. The Federalists supported the new Constitution and the strong national government it created. The Democratic-Republicans wanted to prevent the national government from weakening the rights of citizens and the states. Though Samuel Adams had supported the Constitution, he now became a leader of the Democratic-Republicans in Massachusetts.

new system favored the interests of the wealthy and powerful instead of average citizens.

In 1788, Adams was chosen to attend the convention that debated whether Massachusetts should ratify the Constitution. At the convention, Adams listened carefully to all the arguments for and against the Constitution. He saw that many people in Boston supported the Constitution. In the end, he decided to support it. But Adams said the states should add a bill of rights. Other political leaders across the country also called for this added protection of certain important freedoms. Adams especially wanted to add the important point that the states keep all powers not directly given to the new national government. The states eventually approved the U.S. Bill of Rights in 1791.

While attending the Massachusetts convention, Adams was devastated by the death of his son, Samuel, on January 17, 1788. The younger Adams had been a military surgeon throughout the Revolution, and his wartime service left him weak and sickly. Adams soon learned that his son had left him money in his will. The sum of £1,200 (worth about $100,000 today) was the most cash Adams had ever received at one time.

Gradually, Samuel Adams and John Hancock resumed their old friendship. Hancock and Adams had similar views on the Constitution, and in 1789 they ran together for political office. Hancock was

Most political meetings in Boston were held at Faneuil Hall.

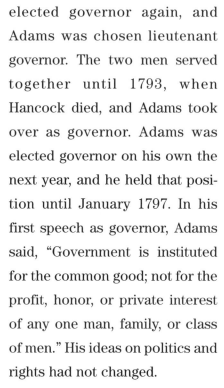

Samuel Adams was concerned about the rights of every person in the United States— even slaves. Unlike most political leaders of the time, he opposed slavery and called on Massachusetts to stop the sale of slaves. When he himself received the gift of a slave in the 1760s, he immediately freed her, although she did stay with his family as a cook.

elected governor again, and Adams was chosen lieutenant governor. The two men served together until 1793, when Hancock died, and Adams took over as governor. Adams was elected governor on his own the next year, and he held that position until January 1797. In his first speech as governor, Adams said, "Government is instituted for the common good; not for the profit, honor, or private interest of any one man, family, or class of men." His ideas on politics and rights had not changed.

As governor of Massachusetts, Samuel Adams continued to fight for equal rights for all. He opposed old laws that let wealthy and important people avoid serving in the militia. He continued to support public education. Adams believed that people must be educated in order to make good political decisions and support liberty.

Samuel Adams spent his last years at a house on Boston's Winter Street, which he had bought in 1784. Elizabeth and Hannah took care of him, as his health was sometimes weak. The palsy that first struck Adams as a young man had gotten worse, and his eyesight began to fade, but his mind was still lively. He particularly enjoyed talking with old friends and visiting with his grandchildren, who read to him from books and newspapers. At times, Adams also ventured out of the house and visited local schools. He enjoyed meeting students and seeing them improve themselves through education.

Samuel Adams died at the age of 81.

By the summer of 1803, Adams could no longer take even short walks along Winter Street. The frail old man could barely speak, and when he did his thoughts often did not make sense. Sensing he was close to death, Adams told his family to keep his funeral simple. He would die just as he had lived his life—without any signs of wealth or power. On October 2, 1803, at the age of 81, Samuel Adams died at his home in Boston.

In the past historians believed that Samuel Adams somehow worked crowds into a frenzy and led protests on his own. Even during his lifetime, some people gave Adams more credit than he deserved.

In 1775, a British soldier in Boston wrote that "this immense continent, from New England to Georgia, is moved and directed by one man!"—Samuel Adams.

A statue of Samuel Adams stands proudly in front of Faneuil Hall in Boston, Massachusetts.

In truth, many Americans had their own reasons for hating the British and wanting independence. They did not blindly follow Adams's every order. And not just one, but many leaders stepped up to fight for liberty.

Adams did play a remarkable role, however. At the time of his death, a local newspaper praised him as the father of the American Revolution. Samuel Adams never fought on the battlefield. But in the war of opinions and ideas, he led the fight for American independence. ॐ

ADAMS'S LIFE

1740
Graduates from
Harvard College with
bachelor's degree

1743
Receives master's
degree from
Harvard College

1722
September 27,
Samuel Adams is
born in Boston,
Massachusetts

1720

1738
Englishman John
Wesley and his brother
Charles found the
Methodist church

1742
The Celsius scale is
developed in Sweden

WORLD EVENTS

1747

Boston town
meeting elects
Adams as clerk;
Adams and some
friends form a
political club

1749

Marries Elizabeth
Checkley on October 1

1764

Writes a statement
protesting the Sugar
Act and Parliament's
right to tax the
colonies; marries
Elizabeth "Betsy"
Wells on December 6

1750

1749

German writer
Johann Wolfgang
Goethe is born

1756-1763

The Seven Years' War
is fought; Britain
defeats France

ADAMS'S LIFE

1765

Massachusetts elects
Adams to the General
Court; Adams writes
resolutions attacking
the Stamp Act

1767

Parliament passes the
Townshend Acts,
which Adams
opposes

1770

British soldiers kill
five colonists during
the Boston Massacre;
Adams convinces
Governor Hutchinson
to send British troops
out of the city

1765

1770

1768

British explorer
Captain James Cook
leaves England for a
three-year exploration
of the Pacific

1770

Clergyman and
chemist Joseph
Priestly gives rubber
its name when he
discovers it rubs
out pencil marks

WORLD EVENTS

1772

Calls for the colonies to form committees of correspondence to discuss British policies and how to change them

1773

Helps organize the Boston Tea Party, protesting a tax on tea

1774

Represents Massachusetts at the First Continental Congress

1772

Poland is partitioned for the first time, between Russia, Prussia, and Austria

1774

King Louis XV of France dies and his grandson, Louis XVI is crowned

ADAMS'S LIFE

1775

Revolutionary War begins, April 19; Adams attends the Second Continental Congress

1776

Signs the Declaration of Independence

1779

Helps write a new constitution for Massachusetts

1775

1776

Scottish economist Adam Smith publishes *The Wealth of Nations*, heralding the beginning of modern economics

1783

Joseph Michel and Jacques Étienne Montgolfier become the first human beings to fly with their invention of the hot air balloon

WORLD EVENTS

1793

John Hancock dies; Adams takes over as governor of Massachusetts until his retirement in 1797

1788

Supports the U.S. Constitution; calls for a Bill of Rights, which is approved in 1791

1803

October 2, dies at his home in Boston, Massachusetts

1790

1789

The French Revolution begins with the storming of the Bastille prison in Paris

1801

Ultraviolet radiation is discovered

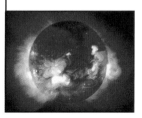

DATE OF BIRTH: September 27, 1722

BIRTHPLACE: Boston, Massachusetts

FATHER: Samuel Adams Sr.
(1698-1748)

MOTHER: Mary Fifield Adams
(1694-1748)

EDUCATION: Harvard College
(B.A. and M.A.)

FIRST SPOUSE: Elizabeth Checkley
(1725-1757); married
October 1, 1749

CHILDREN: Samuel Adams
(born and died 1750)
Samuel Adams
(1751-1788)
Joseph Adams
(born and died 1753)
Mary Adams
(born and died 1754)
Hannah Adams Wells
(1756-1821)
Infant Adams
(stillborn 1757)

SECOND SPOUSE: Elizabeth Wells
(1735-1808); married
December 6, 1764

DATE OF DEATH: October 2, 1803

PLACE OF BURIAL: Granary Burial Ground,
Boston

In the Library

Bohannon, Lisa Frederiksen. *The American Revolution*. Minneapolis: Lerner Publications, 2004.

Hossell, Karen Price. *The Boston Tea Party*. Chicago: Heinemann Library, 2003.

Hull, Mary. *Shays' Rebellion and the Constitution in American History*. Berkeley Heights, N.J.: Enslow Publishers, 2000.

Irvin, Benjamin. *Samuel Adams: Son of Liberty, Father of Revolution*. New York: Oxford Press, 2002.

Jones, Veda Boyd. *Samuel Adams: Patriot*. Philadelphia: Chelsea House Publishers, 2002.

Williams, Jean Kinney. *The U.S. Constitution*. Minneapolis: Compass Point Books, 2004.

On the Web

For more information on *Samuel Adams*, use FactHound to track down Web sites related to this book.

1. Go to *www.facthound.com*
2. Type in a search word related to this book or this book ID: 0756508231
3. Click on the *Fetch It* button.

FactHound will find the best Web sites for you.

Historical Sites

Boston Historical Society and Museum
Old State House
206 Washington St.
Boston, MA 02109-1713
617/ 720-1713
To learn more about the Revolutionary War and its participants

Independence Hall
Independence National Historical Park
143 S. Third St.
Philadelphia, PA 19106
To see where Samuel Adams and other leaders signed the Declaration of Independence

bayonet
a blade attached to the end of a rifle and used as a weapon in close combat

boycott
a refusal to buy certain goods or services as a form of protest

Constitution
the document stating the basic laws of the United States

duties
taxes on goods brought into a country

federal
having to do with the central government of the United States

militia
a loosely organized military force, often made up of local volunteers

morals
a person's beliefs about what is right and wrong

palsy
a health condition marked by uncontrollable shaking of the body or a part of the body

Parliament
the part of the British government that makes laws

patriots
American colonists who wanted their independence from Britain

ratify
to agree to; to approve officially

smuggling
bringing goods into a country illegally

Chapter 1

Page 10, line 1: Harry Alonzo Cushing, ed. *The Writings of Samuel Adams, Volume 3.* New York: G. P. Putnam's Sons, 1906, p. 171.

Chapter 2

Page 23, line 14: William M. Fowler Jr. *Samuel Adams: Radical Puritan.* New York: Longman, 1997, p. 25.

Chapter 3

Page 28, line 25: Paul Lewis. *The Grand Incendiary: A Biography of Samuel Adams.* New York: Dial Press, 1973, p. 17.

Page 31, line 21: William V. Wells. *The Life and Public Services of Samuel Adams, Volume 1.* Reprint ed. Freeport, N.Y.: Books for Libraries Press, 1969, p. 25.

Page 33, line 5: Stewart Beach. *Samuel Adams: The Fateful Years, 1764-1776.* New York: Dodd, Mead & Company, 1965, p. 13.

Page 33, line 13: Pauline Maier. *The Old Revolutionaries: Political Lives in the Age of Samuel Adams.* New York: Alfred A. Knopf, 1980, p. 34.

Chapter 4

Page 37, line 27: *The Life and Public Services of Samuel Adams,* p. 48.

Page 42, line 25: John K. Alexander. *Samuel Adams: America's Revolutionary Politician.* Lanham, Md.: Rowman & Littlefield Publishers, Inc., 2002, p. 28.

Page 45, line 25: *The Writings of Samuel Adams, Volume 1,* p. 164.

Chapter 5

Page 52, line 11: *Samuel Adams: The Fateful Years,* p. 167.

Page 54, line 8: *Samuel Adams: America's Revolutionary Politician,* p. 82.

Page 56, line 15: Ibid., p. 213.

Page 58, line 7: *The Grand Incendiary: A Biography of Samuel Adams,* p. 151.

Page 60, line 4: *Samuel Adams: The Fateful Years, 1764-1776,* p. 252.

Page 61, line 5: *The Writings of Samuel Adams,* p. 76.

Page 61, line 11: "A Shoemaker and the Tea Party." *History Matters.* http://historymatters.gmu.edu/d/5799/

Page 62, line 29: Henry Steele Commager and Morris, Richard B., eds. *The Spirit of 'Seventy-Six.* New York: Harper & Row, 1967, p. 35.

Chapter 6

Page 66, line 23: *Samuel Adams: The Fateful Years, 1764-1776*, p. 264.

Page 67, line 5: *The Spirit of 'Seventy-Six*, p. 50.

Page 67, sidebar: *Samuel Adams: America's Revolutionary Politician*, p. 143.

Page 70, line 14: *The Spirit of 'Seventy-Six*, p. 61.

Chapter 7

Page 79, lines 9, 18: Garry Wills. *Inventing America: Jefferson's Declaration of Independence.* New York: Vintage Books, 1978, p. 22.

Page 80, line 4: Harry Alonzo Cushing, ed. *The Writings of Samuel Adams, Volume 3.* New York: G. P. Putnam's Sons, 1906, p. 297.

Page 80, lines 8, 10: Saul K. Padover, ed. *The World of the Founding Fathers.* New York: Thomas Yoseloff, 1960, p. 104.

Page 81, line 11: *Samuel Adams: America's Revolutionary Politician*, p. 163.

Page 82, line 16: "Constitution of Massachusetts, 1780." *National Humanities Institute.* The Center for Constitutional Studies. http://www.nhinet.org/ccs/docs/ma-1780.htm

Chapter 8

Page 85, line 10: William V. Wells. *The Life and Public Services of Samuel Adams, Volume 3.* Reprint ed. Freeport, N.Y.: Books for Libraries Press, 1969, p. 138.

Page 92, line 11: William V. Wells. *The Life and Public Services of Samuel Adams, Volume 4.* Reprint ed. Freeport, N.Y.: Books for Libraries Press, 1969, p. 357.

Page 94, line 1: *The Old Revolutionaries: Political Lives in the Age of Samuel Adams*, p. 17.

Alexander, John K. *Samuel Adams: America's Revolutionary Politician.* Lanham, Md.: Rowman & Littlefield Publishers, Inc., 2002.

Beach, Stewart. *Samuel Adams: The Fateful Years, 1764-1776.* New York: Dodd, Mead & Company, 1965.

Canfield, Cass. *Sam Adams's Revolution (1765-1776).* New York: Harper & Row, 1976.

Commager, Henry Steele, and Richard B. Morris, eds. *The Spirit of 'Seventy-Six.* New York: Harper & Row, 1967.

Cushing, Harry Alonzo, ed. *The Writings of Samuel Adams, Volumes 1–4.* New York: G. P. Putnam's Sons, 1906.

Faragher, John Mack, ed. *The Encyclopedia of Colonial and Revolutionary America.* New York: Da Capo Press, 1996.

Fleming, Thomas. *Liberty!: The American Revolution.* New York: Viking, 1997.

Fowler, William M., Jr. *Samuel Adams: Radical Puritan.* New York: Longman, 1997.

Lewis, Paul. *The Grand Incendiary: A Biography of Samuel Adams.* New York: Dial Press, 1973.

Library of Congress

Locke, John. *The Second Treatise of Government.* Indianapolis: Bobb-Merrill Educational Publishing, 1952.

Maier, Pauline. *The Old Revolutionaries: Political Lives in the Age of Samuel Adams.* New York: Alfred A. Knopf, 1980.

Padover, Saul K., ed. *The World of the Founding Fathers.* New York: Thomas Yoseloff, 1960.

Unger, Harlow Giles. *John Hancock: Merchant King and American Patriot.* New York: John Wiley & Sons, 2000.

U.S. National Archives and Records Administration

U.S. Congressional Documents and Debates, 1774-1875, *Journals of the Continental Congress*

Wells, William V. *The Life and Public Services of Samuel Adams.* Reprint ed. Freeport, N.Y.: Books for Libraries Press, 1969.

Wills, Garry. *Inventing America: Jefferson's Declaration of Independence.* New York: Vintage Books, 1978.

Michael Burgan is a freelance writer of books for children and adults. A history graduate of the University of Connecticut, he has written more than 60 fiction and nonfiction children's books for various publishers. For adult audiences, he has written news articles, essays, and plays. Michael Burgan is a recipient of an Educational Press Association of America award and belongs to the Society of Children's Book Writers and Illustrators.